ALSO BY ARNOLD WEINSTEIN

A Scream Goes Through the House: What Literature Teaches Us About Life

Vision and Response in Modern Fiction

Fictions of the Self: 1550–1800

The Fiction of Relationship

Nobody's Home: Speech, Self, and Place in American Fiction from Hawthorne to DeLillo